PROJECT-BASED LEARNING IN SCIENCE™

EXPLORING JOURNAL WRITING

THROUGH SCIENCE RESEARCH PROJECTS

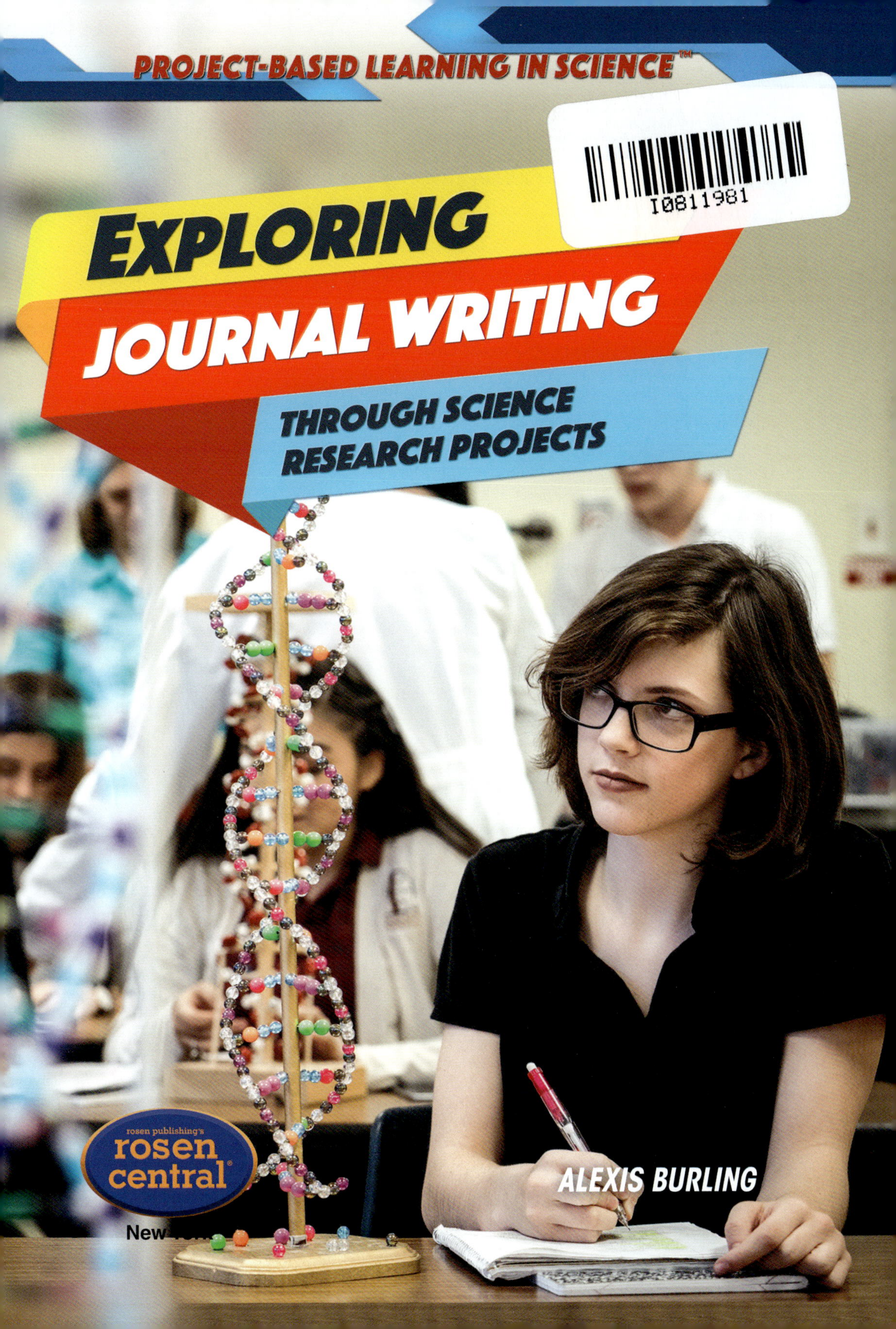

ALEXIS BURLING

rosen publishing's rosen central®

New

Published in 2019 by The Rosen Publishing Group, Inc.
29 East 21st Street, New York, NY 10010

First Edition

Library of Congress Cataloging-in-Publication Data

Names: Burling, Alexis, author.
Title: Exploring journal writing through science research projects / Alexis Burling.
Description: First edition. | New York: Rosen Central, 2019 | Series: Project-based learning in science | Audience: Grades 5–8. | Includes bibliographic references and index.
Identifiers: LCCN 2018010589| ISBN 9781508184782 (library bound) | ISBN 9781508184775 (pbk.)
Subjects: LCSH: Communication in science—Juvenile literature. | Technical writing—Juvenile literature. | Science projects—Juvenile literature.
Classification: LCC Q179.94 .B87 2018 | DDC 808.06/65—dc23
LC record available at https://lccn.loc.gov/2018010589

Manufactured in the United States of America

CONTENTS

INTRODUCTION

Marie Curie is one of the most remarkable women in the history of science. She was the first woman to win a Nobel Prize, the first person to win two Nobel Prizes, and the only woman to win a Nobel Prize in two different fields—physics and chemistry. She also discovered two chemical elements, polonium and radium.

Born Maria Sklodowska on November 7, 1867, in Warsaw, Poland, Curie spent most of her career tinkering in a laboratory. Alongside her husband, Pierre Curie, she conducted hundreds of experiments to study a mysterious type of energy given off by matter in the form of waves or high-speed particles. She called this energy radiation.

During Curie's time, most scientists were still unclear about what radiation was and what it could do. But today, it is well known that radiation can be used in many ways to help humankind. For example, dentists use radiation to take X-rays of your teeth before a cleaning. Doctors treat cancer patients with small doses of radiation in order to shrink harmful tumors. Thanks to the Curies' efforts, the use of radiation has led to advances in other areas too, including agriculture, geology, space exploration, and archeology.

Marie Curie's discoveries changed the way humans thought about the world. But she would not have accomplished such breakthroughs without keeping meticulously documented records of her work that she could go back and reference. These scientific journals contained her research notes, sketches, and detailed accounts of her successes and failures. After her death in 1934, Curie's journals provided proof of her tireless work ethic and all that she had learned. In time, they also became a library's worth of information upon which future scientists could build.

In 1906, Marie Curie became the first woman to serve on the faculty of the Sorbonne, the top university in Paris, France.

Professional scientists like Curie are not the only ones who keep journals. As a budding scientist, you can—and should—too! Keeping a science journal is a great way to take control of the learning process. It will help you understand how real-world problems can be solved. The practice has many proven benefits. It boosts your writing and communication skills. It helps you keep track of your thought processes. Plus, your journal can be anything you want it to be. It might be a collection of observations about what's going on in class or your reactions to an interesting field trip. If you're doing a science experiment, it's also the perfect place to write down your hypotheses, ask

Science journals are especially helpful when you're doing lab experiments. You can keep track of measurements, draw charts or graphs, and record detailed notes.

questions, draw graphs and charts, or include photographs, diagrams, and even pressed samples from the field.

The best way to find out more about why a science journal is useful is through the lens of project-based learning. Project-based learning is an exciting way of teaching that enables students to dive deeper into the learning experience by coming up with research- and experiment-based projects and following them through to completion. If this sounds boring, think again! Project-based learning in science inspires students to contemplate the wonders of the universe and ask why or how on their own terms.

In the following chapters, you'll find a series of prompts that ask questions about various concepts found in physical science, life science, Earth and space science, and engineering design. Each prompt has a corresponding experiment or project you can do to explore the ideas in greater detail and help you figure out the answer (or answers) to the prompt. You can also use the projects listed in the book as models to design your own project-based learning experiment.

Every project in this book is up to your interpretation—and fun. Keep in mind that there are also multiple kinds of investigations you can do. In controlled investigations, you plan and carry out experiments to manipulate the variable being studied. Field investigations study a natural or human-made environment and form hypotheses about the plants or animals that live there. Design experiments use your understanding of scientific principles to design and construct a product that meets a need in society. Secondary research investigations use research or data obtained by others to answer a question. Some of the projects require working on your own, while others are better suited for working as a team.

No matter how many projects you try or create, it's important to approach each one with an open mind. Don't forget to make good use of your journal during the process. After all, you could be the next Marie Curie!

CHAPTER ONE

LEARNING ABOUT PHYSICAL SCIENCE

Take a look around you. Do you ever wonder what's keeping your school bus rooted to the ground on the way to school? When you throw a ball up in the air, why does it *always* come down? What causes the changes that objects go through when they burn, rot, or rust? All of these questions can be answered by people who specialize in physical science.

Physical science concerns the study of the inorganic, or nonliving, world. Throughout history, physical scientists such as Marie Curie, Robert Boyle, Isaac Newton, and Galileo Galilei worked in laboratories and did experiments to uncover mind-boggling truths about the way the universe functions. They focused on what matter is and how energy works.

One major branch of physical science is physics. In the broadest terms, physics focuses on matter and motion. It explores topics like heat, light, electricity, sound, mechanics, and magnetism. Physicists study everything from the structure and behavior of atoms to Earth's gravitational pull.

The other major branch of physical science is chemistry. Chemistry examines the composition, structure, and properties of everyday substances, as well as how elements and molecules interact and change to form new substances. Like physics, chemistry touches every aspect of our lives. The air we breathe, the objects we use in school, and even the food we eat are all products of chemical reactions in some way.

Robert Boyle conducted hundreds of lab experiments. Between 1647 and 1691, he filled approximately forty work diaries with chemical recipes, measurements, and data sets.

QUESTION: HOW DOES THE RELATIONSHIP BETWEEN THE VOLUME OF A GAS AND PRESSURE ON AN OBJECT INFLUENCE THE DISTANCE THE OBJECT TRAVELS WHEN FORCE IS APPLIED?

Robert Boyle was one of the greatest thinkers of the scientific revolution (mid-1500s–1700). Born in Ireland in 1627, he is often called the father of chemistry by historians because he pioneered many groundbreaking discoveries. Perhaps the most famous discovery was Boyle's law, which explains the inverse relationship between the pressure and volume of a gas.

In the mid-seventeenth century, Boyle began studying the pressure and volume of a confined gas when held at a constant temperature. Using the scientific method, he did a number of experiments and took notes in his journals. He included charts, graphs, and sketches of the tools he used.

THE SCIENTIFIC METHOD

Most scientists perform experiments for three reasons: to answer a question, to solve a problem, and to further knowledge. Like Robert Boyle, they do so by completing a series of steps called the scientific method. An experiment is considered successful when it can be replicated by the original scientist or by others. To achieve success, follow these steps when conducting any science experiment:

- **Ask a question** about the world around you.
- **Do background research** using books, the internet, or other forms of media. You can also interview an expert.
- **Form a hypothesis**, which is an educated guess based on observation.
- **Design and complete an experiment** to test your hypothesis.
- **Collect and record data** in your journal. Create charts and graphs to analyze the data.
- **Form a conclusion.** Decide whether the experiment worked. Was your hypothesis correct?
- **Reflect on the experiment and communicate results.** If you could do the experiment over again, what would you do differently? Did the experiment raise new questions? If necessary, do a new experiment to further your research.

In one experiment, he took a J-shaped tube called a manometer that was sealed on one end and filled with air. Then, he poured mercury into the tube, which displaced the air at a proportional rate. The more mercury he poured in, the more air was pushed out. When he doubled the pressure by pouring in double the amount of mercury, the air shrank to half its original volume. Therefore, Boyle realized that the volume of a gas was inversely proportional to the amount of pressure being exerted on it as long as the temperature remained constant. The breakthrough became known as Boyle's law.

PROJECT
POP! GOES THE POTATO CANNON

Boyle's law is interesting in theory, but it's even more fascinating (and explosive!) in practice. Construct a potato cannon to see it in action. Analyze what happens when force is applied on an object in a partially enclosed and pressurized space.

- *Gather supplies. You'll need a piece of PVC pipe about 2 or 3 feet (61–91 centimeters) long with a 1-inch (2.5 cm) diameter, several potatoes, a dowel rod (or similarly shaped object), and a measuring tape. Don't forget to wear goggles during the experiment to protect your eyes.*
- *First, create potato cores by pushing the PVC pipe through the potato.*
- *Next, write down some predictions in your journal about what you think might happen*

If pushing the potatoes onto the PVC pipe to make potato cores proves too difficult, ask an adult for help. Or you can cut the potato into small-enough pieces using a knife.

when you push one potato core through the tube. How far do you think it will go? Then predict what might happen when you add a second potato core to the mix. Do you think it will travel further?

- *Now, go outside and do the experiment. Using the dowel rod, push one potato core through the tube and measure how far it went. Write down the results.*
- *Then do the experiment using two potato cores. Place one potato core into each end*

of the PVC pipe. Using the dowel rod, gently push the potato closest to you toward the potato core at the other end of the pipe, until it reaches halfway. Now push the dowel rod into the first potato core again using some force. Measure how far each of the potato cores flew and write down in your science journal the distance they each traveled.

- *If you have the available materials, try the experiment again using different-sized pipes and potato pieces or balls. As always, keep track of your progress in your journal. Present your findings to the class in a video or in-person demonstration.*

QUESTION: IN WHAT WAYS ARE NEWTON'S LAWS OF MOTION DEMONSTRATED IN TODAY'S MODERN WORLD?

Isaac Newton was another important scientist who lived during the scientific revolution. He helped formulate the major principles of modern physics. He invented a reflecting telescope in 1663. He also studied mathematics and astronomy. But he is best known for coming up with three laws of motion.

Newton's first law of motion states that a moving or stationary body will keep moving or stay stationary unless an external force is applied to it. For example, a car will keep moving unless it smashes into a brick wall. A ball will remain still on your kitchen table unless you give it a push. This is sometimes also called the law of inertia.

Watch out! This mischievous kitty is about to demonstrate Newton's first law of motion. That dish of tasty treats will stay still until the cat swipes it off the table.

Newton's second law of motion explains that when an object is acted on by an outside force, the strength of that force is equal to the object's mass times its acceleration (force = mass × acceleration). A change in speed is proportional to the force applied. For example, if you drop a penny and a boulder from your roof at school, they will fall at the same rate. But the boulder will make a greater impact because its mass is larger than the penny's.

Finally, Newton's third law of motion states that for every action, there is an equal and opposite reaction. For example, imagine pushing your feet against the wall of a swimming pool. When you push against the pool's wall, your body will float off in the opposite direction, away from the wall.

Video cameras are a great way to document research when in the field. Most smartphones have video apps, too.

PROJECT
LOCAL MOTION

Evidence of Newton's laws of motion is everywhere. But how are they relevant? Observe these patterns in nature to analyze the relationship between force, mass, and acceleration in your daily life. Then use your creative brain to construct a physical model of what you learned. This project can be done alone or with a partner.

- *Choose which one of Newton's three laws of motion to focus on.*
- *Now go explore your neighborhood. It can be the area where you live, where your parent or guardian works, or where you go to school. In your journal, make a list of all the instances where you see Newton's law taking place. If you have access to a smartphone or a camera, take video clips, too!*

- *Pick one example and build a model for the class that re-creates Newton's law of motion. It can be a demonstration using two separate objects or a new type of contraption that you construct out of everyday materials found at school or home. Use your imagination! Don't forget to use your journal to sketch out any diagrams or images that might help you build your model and document your progress.*
- *Then present your model to the class. After you're done, lead a group discussion about what would happen if Newton's law suddenly stopped working. How would your model be affected? What would be the impact on society?*

QUESTION: WHY DO SOME FRUITS DECAY FASTER THAN OTHERS WHEN EXPOSED TO AIR?

All matter is composed of tiny particles called atoms and molecules that are constantly in motion. Sometimes these atoms and molecules interact with each other and cause chemical reactions. A common (and potentially gross-looking or bad-smelling) example is when food spoils.

It is natural for food to decay. But the process is aided by a number of factors, including air, light, temperature, and exposure to moisture. For instance, too much moisture in the air can cause a microorganism called mold to grow on a slice of bread. When a cut avocado is exposed to oxygen, it oxidizes quickly and turns brown. If lettuce sits in the hot sun for too long, its leaves will dry up and become discolored because of a process called photodegradation.

All of these problems can be prevented—or at least delayed—by refrigeration and by using modern inventions such as plastic wrap.

PROJECT
SPOILED ROTTEN

Are you curious to find out more about the chemistry behind food spoilage? Conduct a controlled experiment using different pieces of fruit to determine which factors have the greatest impact on the rate of decay. You should consider the following: oxygen, light exposure, moisture exposure, refrigeration, length of time, and temperature.

- *Take a look in your refrigerator. Pick three to five fruits to study over a monthlong period. Some ideas include a whole grape, half an avocado (with the pit included), an apple, or a banana. Place one piece of each fruit on a windowsill and one piece of the same fruit in the refrigerator.*
- *In your journal, describe how each fruit looks. You can include drawings, photographs, and measurements. Be sure to differentiate whether the fruit you're describing is in the refrigerator or on the windowsill. If it's on the sill, make note of how much sunlight is coming through the window, if at all. Then write down your predictions. Ask yourself: How long will each fruit stay fresh? What*

Fruit reacts to light, air, moisture, and a lack of refrigeration in different ways. Tomatoes and lemons grow mold. Bananas get mushy and develop brown spots on their peels.

physical changes might take place over time? Will the fruit change color? Will it grow mold?

- *Now observe each fruit over the course of a month. Keep track of the changes taking place in your journal using notes, sketches, or photographs. Write down how long it takes for each piece of fruit to decay. If the fruit starts to smell or attract flies, throw it out. You don't want a fruit fly infestation!*
- *Finally, find out what happened to each piece of fruit by doing some research. Compare and contrast your results and create a presentation for the class. If you're feeling artistic, create a poster using the notes and sketches from your journal. Include an infographic, if possible. Show and tell is encouraged.*

CHAPTER TWO

LEARNING ABOUT LIFE SCIENCE

Life science is the study of living things, such as plants, animals, and human beings. For thousands of years, scientists such as Aristotle, Charles Darwin, Rachel Carson, and Jane Goodall have laid the foundation for what we now know to be true in the field of life science.

One of the major branches of life science is biology. It is defined as the study of life and how living things survive and change. Some of the many other areas of life sciences include zoology (the study of animals), entomology (the study of bugs), and botany (the study of plants).

Life scientists study the big and the miniscule, the concrete and the abstract. Microbiologists investigate tiny, microscopic organisms so small you need a microscope to see them. Ecologists think about how living things impact or interact with their environment. Geneticists examine hereditary traits, while paleontologists dig up fossils and contemplate the history of life on Earth. It's an extraordinary field, and the opportunity for life scientists to uncover new ideas through field research, lab work, and hands-on experiments is seemingly endless.

QUESTION: WHAT CAN YOU LEARN BY USING A MICROSCOPE?

Scientists use microscopes to study things that cannot be seen with the human eye. While there are several types of microscopes, the kind most commonly used in schools or by young scientists is the optical microscope. This kind of microscope uses light, mirrors, and lenses to provide a magnified look at something. The specimens, or objects being viewed, are usually placed on

Melanin is a pigment that gives human skin, hair, and eyes their color. It protects against the sun's ultraviolet rays. Dark-haired people have more melanin in their hair than light-haired people do.

slides. A slide is a thin rectangle made of glass or another see-through material.

One of the many things you can observe using a microscope is hair. Human hair comes in many colors, such as blond, brown, red, and black. It can be curly, straight, or somewhere in between. Hair color comes from a substance called melanin. The lighter your hair, the less melanin it has. The same goes for skin.

Hair is formed when a group of living cells join together beneath the skin to create a protein called keratin. Hair starts at the root and grows through a tube in the skin called a follicle. When hair reaches the outside of the skin, the cells inside each strand die. That's why it doesn't hurt when you get a haircut!

Most people have about one hundred thousand hairs on their head at any given time. But humans lose about fifty to one hundred hairs a day during combing or washing. One perplexing question that still has life scientists stumped is why some people lose more hair than others. Why do some people go bald at an early age while others still have a full head of hair at age eighty? Is it possible to prevent hair loss? Life scientists use microscopes to study aspects of this and other physical ailments or illnesses in order to get to the root of the problem and figure out a solution that lasts.

PROJECT
IT'S THERE IN YOUR HAIR!

The human body is made up of blood, organs, and billions of cells that are so small they can be viewed only under a microscope. What's also fascinating is seeing how each strand of hair is different! Do this experiment to witness the magic with your own eyes. Then use the notes you took in

Including slide drawings in your science journal is the perfect way to document all the atoms and molecules you see when using a microscope.

your science journal to create an artistic masterpiece!

- *Gather your materials. You'll need a microscope, five plain glass slides with coverslips, tweezers, scissors, and a small dropper with water.*
- *Pick five pieces of hair from different places. It can be your own hair, a pet's hair, a friend's hair, or a family member's hair. Try using a hair that has been dyed, conditioned, or frequently styled with a hair dryer or curling iron. Cut each piece of hair down to ½ inch (1.25 cm) so it will fit on the slide without falling off. Put a droplet of water on each slide so that the hair will stay in place. Using the tweezers, place each piece of hair on a different slide with its own coverslip on top.*
- *Now look at each hair under the microscope. What do you see? Can you see a difference between each type of hair? Does it make a difference if the hair has been heat treated?*

Frequently dyed? Take notes and make initial sketches in your journal.

- *Now create larger-than-life paintings of each slide as seen from the microscope. Make sure you note the edges of each piece of hair and any bumps or tears. If you're working in a group, have each group member do a different painting. Create a gallery of your drawings.*

QUESTION: HOW DO DIFFERENCES IN STRUCTURE AND/OR FUNCTION INFLUENCE BIODIVERSITY AMONG LIVING THINGS AND ORGANISMS' ABILITY TO REPRODUCE AND SURVIVE?

Charles Darwin was an English biologist and geologist who lived during the nineteenth century. In 1859, he published *On the Origin of Species*. The book described a theory of evolution that was revolutionary at the time but became the foundation on which most of Western life science is based.

Darwin hypothesized that species evolved because of a process he called natural selection. He argued that species change over time because the members of a species that have traits that make it easier for them to survive will be more likely to live long enough to reproduce. For example, if some salamanders have a camouflage pattern that makes them harder to see, they are less likely to be eaten by predators. More of these salamanders will live long enough to have babies, who are likely to inherit this same camouflage pattern. Darwin called this cycle "the survival of the fittest."

Earth is full of ecosystems—communities of plants, animals, and other organisms. The organisms in an ecosystem compete for

FROM A TO Z

When Charles Darwin was doing research on his theory of evolution, he traveled around the world on a ship. Whether he was on board or off, he kept detailed notes from the field in leather-bound, pocket-sized notebooks. He wrote vertically down the page, in pencil. Sometimes he made graphs or maps, included barometer readings, drew detailed sketches of animals or bugs, or pressed plant specimens onto the pages.

Charles Darwin took twenty years to write and perfect *On the Origin of Species* before the book was published.

Upon his return, Darwin continued his work on evolution and produced even more notebooks, this time writing in pen. Sometimes he started at both ends and worked toward the middle. He labeled these notebooks using the letters of the alphabet. He also printed his name and address inside each one in case it got lost.

resources, such as food, water, and a place to live. Those with traits most adapted to their particular ecosystem—such as plants that need less water in a desert—are most likely to survive. Over time, if only the organisms with this trait survive in the ecosystem, they may evolve into a separate species.

PROJECT
MY DIVERSE NEIGHBORHOOD

The world is a diverse place—and there is a lot of competition for resources. Explore your backyard or neighborhood to learn more about the ecosystems that have taken root there. Use your eyes and ears to theorize why the plants, animals, and even humans there have survived while others have died out.

- *Take a stroll in your backyard or around your neighborhood. Don't forget to bring your journal! Write down a list of what you see and hear. Take note of the bugs, trees, plants, animals, birds, and inorganic objects. Drawings, illustrations, photographs, and even leaf rubbings are encouraged. Observe the same place over a period of weeks or months to see how the animals, plants, and insects interact.*
- *Then pick a way to introduce others to the ecosystem you witnessed. You could make a poster showing the food web that connects the species you observed, some other artistic visual (such as a diorama), or even a video documentary charting your walkabouts over the course of your observations. Don't forget to consider how humans have played a role*

Flowers smell wonderful, especially in springtime. How do their smells affect and often help bees, birds, and other living things in their ecosystem?

in the ecosystem—both detrimental and beneficial.

- Now channel Charles Darwin and hypothesize which organisms in your ecosystem are dominant because of their ability to adapt and which are likely to die out if weather conditions change or when food becomes scarce. Pick one particularly well-equipped plant, animal, or human and write a poem or song about its success. Include details about its inherited beneficial traits. Present your handiwork to the class, along with the poster, diorama, or video you created in the second stage of the experiment.

Question: How does the amount of compost (organic material) in a soil mixture and the degree of fertilization affect the germination and growth of certain plants when planted from seed?

As with any living thing, plants need energy to grow. They get energy by making their own food. To do this, plants need water (which they absorb from wet soil, mostly through their roots), carbon dioxide (which they get from the air), and sunlight. The process of converting these three things into food is called photosynthesis.

Here's how photosynthesis works. Plants' leaves are made of tiny holes that take in carbon dioxide from the air. The leaves also contain molecules called chlorophyll. Chlorophyll absorbs energy from the sun, which breaks apart the water that has been absorbed through the plant's stem. When the water mixes with the carbon dioxide, a sugar called glucose is formed. Plants use glucose for food.

In addition to light and regular watering, plants need healthy soil in order to survive. Basic soil is composed of a mixture of dirt, sand, and rock. But many expert gardeners add compost to soil to help plants grow. Compost is made of important nutrients, minerals, and organic matter—the decaying remains of animals and plants. Some gardeners use soil that comes with compost mixed in. Others add their own homemade compost instead. It can come from broken-down eggshells, fungi, and even worms!

PROJECT
GROW YOUR OWN GARDEN

Grow your favorite vegetable from scratch. Discover what the best growing conditions are for your plant by creating a controlled experiment using different variables. Consider how soil composition and the addition of fertilizer affect the plant's overall growth and health.

Remember to keep track of what the ratio of regular dirt to potting soil is in each of the pots that you use.

- *Choose a vegetable to grow from seed. Go to your local gardening supply store or supermarket and ask which seeds would best suit your purpose. You will also need to pick up some pots, different types of potting soil (including some with added compost), perlite (a type of tiny volcanic rock), and fertilizer.*
- *Now prepare your pots. Each pot should contain a different ratio of compost to regular soil. Also, prepare two identical pots with the same dirt-to-compost ratio. At least one pot should contain perlite, while the control pot should just contain dirt. Write down the soil percentage for each pot in your science journal. Then plant the same number of seeds in each pot.*
- *Place the pots on a windowsill or in another sunny area. You can also put the pots outside. Just make sure the weather won't get too chilly in the day or at night during the growing period. Research how often to water the plants*

or ask an expert gardener for advice. Here's a great place to start: https://kidsgardening .org/gardening-toolbox.

- *Add fertilizer (such as Miracle Grow) to one of the pair of identical pots when watering. This will allow you to compare and contrast the fertilizer's impact on plant growth.*
- *For sixty to ninety days, keep track of each plant's growth in your journal. Include charts, drawings, and measurements. At the end of the growing season, present your findings to the class using a slide show or colorful poster, complete with infographics. If you grew any vegetables, you can also provide a tasty snack for your classmates to munch on.*

CHAPTER THREE

LEARNING ABOUT EARTH AND SPACE SCIENCE

When you look up at the sky at night, it is impossible not to wonder what's out there. Most scientists agree that there are eight planets in our solar system and at least one hundred billion stars in our galaxy. But what exactly is Earth's place in this vast universe? Are there more universes out there? If so, are there other planets like Earth where life can thrive? What makes Earth so special, and how do we keep it healthy?

Over the course of history, people like Ptolemy, Aristotle, Nicolaus Copernicus, Johannes Kepler, Stephen Hawking, and Sylvia Earle have asked similar questions. They work (or worked) in Earth and space science, the study of the physical and ecological systems that affect our planet and the rest of the universe. Several fields are part of Earth and space science. Astronomers observe the behavior of the stars, planets, and other objects in space. Meteorologists examine the Earth's atmosphere to learn how it determines our planet's weather systems and climate. Oceanographers explore the composition, movement, and structure of the world's oceans. Geologists study how natural phenomena like earthquakes, extreme storms, and erosion change the Earth's surface over time.

Earth scientists contemplate how human activities have impacted and continue to affect Earth's development. They investigate complex issues concerning our uses of land, energy, mineral, and water resources and whether we are being smart in our choices. Global climate change is one of the most complicated and pressing problems of our time. Every day, scientists examine Earth's past to better prepare for its future.

QUESTION: WHAT ARE THE PROCESSES THAT SHAPE THE LAND IN YOUR AREA? HOW CAN WE USE PATTERNS TO PREDICT CHANGES ON EARTH'S SURFACE?

When scientists study Earth, they look at four major systems: the geosphere, which is made up of rock, soil, and sediments; the hydrosphere, which is made of water and ice; the biosphere, which contains all living things; and the atmosphere. These four systems interact and impact the way Earth looks and functions in different ways. For example, water covers about 70 percent of the Earth's surface. Oceans support ecosystems within their watery depths, but they also shape landmasses and have an effect on climate.

Lots of other factors affect the way Earth changes over time. Weather (wind, rain, tornadoes, floods, drought) and erosion are two of the biggest influences. Volcanoes can erupt after thousands of years of lying dormant. The shifting and colliding of tectonic plates creates earthquakes. But one of the biggest changes in recent history is the way humans have started using the environment in negative ways. Some examples include

pollution, land misuse, the burning of fossil fuels, and an overconsumption of natural resources. If this behavior is left unchecked, it can lead to the deterioration of natural habitats and the extinction of vulnerable species.

The largest ocean on Earth is the Pacific Ocean. It covers around 30 percent of Earth's surface. The planet's other oceans are the Atlantic, Arctic, Indian, and Southern Oceans.

PROJECT
MY TOWN, THEN AND NOW

Many factors influence the way land is shaped. Conduct field research to analyze how an area in your region has changed over time—for better or for worse. Then brainstorm ways in which the humans you know can make changes to their behavior in order to lessen their footprint and shape the environment in positive ways.

- *Choose an area of your town, city, or region that you want to learn more about. It can be a park, lake, mountain, national monument, or urban area. First, think of questions you want to have answered. Some examples are: How was the land or water in the area used*

Looking at physical, topographic, resource, and road maps from different eras can help you understand how the land in a certain area has changed over time.

over time? What did the area look like in its early history? How has human activity altered the environment? Write down these questions in your journal.

- *Research your area's history to find answers to your questions and record the information in your journal. Ask your teacher or a local librarian about which books, maps, or online resources might be good reference materials to consult.*

- *Now it's time for field research! Observe your area for a length of time—a month, six months, or an amount of your choosing. Take detailed notes about the changes taking place during that time.*
- *Create a presentation for the class using archival photographs or illustrations of your place in its early stages, as well as photographs or drawings taken during the observation period. Hand-drawn maps and infographics are encouraged! Include predictions about what the area will look like in one year, five years, and ten years. Explain what factors influenced your thinking.*
- *At the end of your presentation, lead a class discussion in which you come up with ways to improve the area and lessen the human footprint. If it's a public place or a space run by an organization, find out how to help. It can be through volunteering or by writing a letter to a local newspaper inspiring others to get involved in your cause.*

QUESTION: HOW ARE CHANGES IN EARTH'S WEATHER PATTERNS AND TEMPERATURES AFFECTING OCEAN LIFE, AND HOW DOES THIS RELATE TO GLOBAL WARMING?

According to the National Oceanic and Atmospheric Association's (NOAA) 2017 Global Climate Report, 2016 was the warmest year on record since the NOAA started keeping track in 1880. The 2016 average global temperature across land and ocean surface areas was 1.69 degrees Fahrenheit (0.94 degrees Celsius) higher than the twentieth-century average. A different study referenced in *National Geographic* stated that 2017 was the hottest year on record in terms of ocean heat. What that means is that over a period of decades, the planet has been getting progressively warmer—and the temperature changes are affecting not only weather patterns but also plants and animals and their habitats.

Sylvia Earle (*right*) is one of the world's top oceanographers. Her foundation, Mission Blue, organizes underwater expeditions to help protect and restore fragile oceanic ecosystems.

A nearly two-degree difference doesn't seem like much if you're a human swimming in the ocean. But the creatures that depend on oceanic ecosystems could be in danger. Increased carbon dioxide and declining oxygen levels in some oceans have caused problems for some fish. If they don't find a more hospitable habitat, they will suffocate. Sea ice and ice shelves—especially in the Arctic—are melting, which is causing sea levels to rise. One potentially irreversible problem is coral bleaching. Stressed by pollution and increasing water temperatures, coral have started to expel the algae living in their tissues. Without the algae, coral can starve. Oceanographers such as Sylvia Earle and Jane Lubchenco are working to solve this problem and protect oceanic ecosystems. But there is still more to be done.

PROJECT
HELP SAVE THE OCEANS

Do an experiment to learn how thermohaline circulation works. Then conduct research to find out how global warming is affecting thermohaline circulation and what scientists are doing to solve the problem. Finish by coming up with some of your own solutions.

- *Start by learning more about what thermohaline circulation is. This website is a great place to start: https://pmm.nasa.gov/education/videos/thermohaline-circulation-great-ocean-conveyor-belt.*
- *Then do an experiment. You'll need a quart jar, two eight-ounce glasses, some salt, food coloring, a spoon, and a food thermometer. First, mix four teaspoons of salt in a glass of refrigerated water. Measure the temperature of the water, record the data in your journal, and pour the contents into the jar. This represents the cold oceanic water at the poles. Now mix four teaspoons of salt in a glass of room-temperature water, plus a few drops of food coloring. Measure the temperature of the water and record the data in your journal. This represents the warm, salty oceanic water flowing into the*

polar region. Slowly pour the contents into the jar and observe what happens.

- *Repeat the experiment, using different amounts of salt and temperatures. Write down what happens in your journal, including some analysis of how the experiment illustrates thermohaline circulation.*
- *Now research a specific ocean or part of an ocean in order to hypothesize how global warming is affecting the salinity levels and the health of plants and animals that live there. Here are a few great places to start: https://pmm.nasa.gov/education/videos/thermohaline-circulation-great-ocean-conveyor-belt; https://www.epa.gov/climate-indicators/oceans; and https://oceanservice.noaa.gov/education/tutorial_currents/05conveyor1.html.*
- *Present your findings to the class, using a poster of charts and infographics. Brainstorm ways for humans to get involved and help protect the Earth's oceans. (Hint: Dr. Sylvia Earle has lots of ideas. Look her up!)*

QUESTION: WHAT IDEAL CIRCUMSTANCES NEED TO BE IN PLACE IN ORDER FOR LIFE TO EXIST ON A PLANET?

There are many reasons why nothing lives on Jupiter or Saturn. For one, those planets are made of gas. Mars isn't hospitable to humans either. It's freezing, and the planet's atmosphere is made up of mostly carbon dioxide. But Earth is an ideal place for humans, animals, plants—even microbes and bacteria—to survive and reproduce.

AN OUT-OF-THIS-WORLD DISCOVERY

In November 2017, an article in *Time* reported a fascinating discovery. A team of astronomers had spotted an exoplanet close to our solar system, approximately eleven light-years away from Earth. At about the size of Earth, it orbited its parent star, Ross 128, once every 9.9 days. The astronomers named it Ross 128 b.

Today, scientists are almost certain there aren't living creatures on Ross 128 b. But there are favorable conditions there. Temperatures hover around 73°F (23°C). The planet spins slowly, so it can't fling off an atmosphere if one is in place. And it exists close enough to the red dwarf star Ross 128 to allow liquid water to pool on its surface and potentially support life. Maybe someday scientists will discover there is life there after all!

Earth has a lot going for it. It has a breathable atmosphere consisting of mostly oxygen and nitrogen. It has liquid water, on which most of life depends. It has a magnetic field that protects the planet from extreme radiation or storms of charged particles from the sun. It's the third-closest planet to the sun, which means it's close enough to be warmed by the sun's rays and not too close or far to burn up or freeze. Scientists call Earth's placement in the solar system the Goldilocks Zone. As Goldilocks discovered when she raided the porridge bowls of the three bears, it's not too hot. It's not too cold. It's just right.

PROJECT
THE NEW NINTH PLANET

Imagine and create your own ideal planet where life can exist and flourish.

- *Choose two of your favorite planets (besides Earth). Do some research to find out why life cannot exist there. Consider each planet's placement in the solar system*

You can make your planet as large or as small as you want. But try to make it look different from real planets.

and relationship to the sun, its atmospheric makeup, the structure of each planet's surface area, the percentage of water present, and other criteria.

- *Then imagine a new planet of your own. Think of how it was formed and why it still thrives. What kind of life lives there, and why is that possible? Does it have any moons, rings, or identifying marks? What are its seasons like? The challenge will be to think of a planet that is not an exact replica of Earth.*
- *Now construct a model of your planet using household materials. It can be colorful, soft, or a different shape than any of the existing planets. Create a timeline of how and when your planet formed and a map of where it exists in relation to other planets in our solar system. Show off your planet to the class ... and don't forget to give it a funky name!*

CHAPTER FOUR

LEARNING ABOUT ENGINEERING DESIGN

In 1450, Johannes Gutenberg designed a printing press to mass-produce books and pamphlets so information could be distributed to more people in a shorter amount of time. Alexander Graham Bell came up with the idea for a telephone in the 1880s to help people communicate across distances. For millennia, scientists called engineers have been thinking of ideas for machines and other products that can help solve world problems.

Today, the possibilities—and design opportunities—are becoming more and more advanced. If you lose an arm in an accident, you can get fitted with a mechanical arm that can move and flex much like a human one would. Doctors use 3D printers to create lifelike models of organs in order to practice risky surgeries and explain troubling health conditions to patients. There are driverless cars, elevators that move sideways, glasses that give sight to the blind, and even a newly designed "burger" that looks juicy and red like meat, tastes like meat, but is actually healthier and doesn't involve killing an animal!

This vehicle looks like a normal car. It feels like a regular car, too. But this man is actually sitting in an autonomous vehicle. The car drives itself!

As in any area of science, engineers take into account all the relevant scientific theories and principles when considering their project's potential impact on people and the natural environment. They map out a plan by doing tons of research and learning about what other engineers are doing to solve similar problems. When conducting their own experiments, they pay attention to what works and what doesn't, and they rejigger their designs accordingly until something clicks. Not every idea is successful. In fact, most are flops. But it's the thrill of creation and the promise of progress that keeps most engineers committed to their work.

QUESTION: HOW DOES AN OBJECT'S DESIGN AND STRUCTURE HELP IT SUCCESSFULLY COMPLETE TASKS TO CREATE A BETTER WORLD?

Many objects in nature have specific traits that enable them to fall at a decreasing speed and resist the force of gravity. Think of the seeds that twirl down from the limbs of maple trees. As the seed falls off the tree, it has to stay airborne long enough and

STEP-BY-STEP DESIGN

Designing an original product that works the way you want it to can be tricky. Follow these steps to stay on the right path:

- Identify a need and do background research to learn more about it.
- Brainstorm possible designs for products that might solve the problem. Consider cost, time, and materials you might need.
- Pick one idea and develop a detailed model that can be tested in multiple circumstances.
- Test the design and gather data. If the model can't be built or tested, make a plan to evaluate the design blueprint over time and adjust as necessary.
- Analyze the data and revise the design until success is reached.
- Don't forget to keep track of everything in your journal!

travel far enough away that when it sprouts and grows, the baby tree won't be shaded by its parent. The seeds' propeller-shaped design makes this possible. Nature has solved its own problem.

For this reason, lots of scientists look to nature when working on design projects to help solve real-world issues. One important example is how to transport emergency food, water, and lifesaving medicine to inaccessible areas during wartimes or after a natural disaster. Engineering firms such as DASH Systems in California and even the US Marine Corps have been developing, testing, and retesting designs for flying objects called drones that can be dropped from an airplane without breaking apart.

In September 2017, DASH's Joel Ifill traveled to Puerto Rico after it was devastated by Hurricane Maria. Much of the island was without power, and many roads were flooded or blocked by debris. People needed help—fast. Ifill and his staff used early models of drones to air-drop supplies into the most distraught areas. According to Ifill, the technology will revolutionize the way humanitarian aid is delivered and can help people all over the world. "This is a call to action," he told *Fast Company* magazine. "This is not really about us or our technology, but about using innovation to help our fellow citizens … This is about stepping up to the plate."

PROJECT
SAVE HUMPTY DUMPTY

Design your own indestructible free-falling package! Consider how the container's design and structure influences the rate at which the package falls. How does that influence the likelihood of breakage when dropped from a variety of heights? Work on a team to design and construct the ideal model that will pass the egg-drop test.

Remember to consider the rules of gravity when constructing your design. Think about air-flow, weight, mass, and the speed of acceleration.

- First, take a look at this MythBusters video to see pros in action: https://www.youtube.com/watch?v=ZOMW3hplSpl.
- Now, using household materials of your choosing, design a container that can protect an unboiled egg inside it when dropped from three different heights. Material options include cotton balls, Styrofoam, balloons, rubber bands, and anything else that comes to mind. Think outside the box! Take notes in your journal, including diagrams, drawings, and measurements.
- Conduct the experiment. If your egg breaks, reevaluate your design, make adjustments, and try again for the next-level drop. The winning team in the class is the one whose design withstands the drop from all three heights.

QUESTION: HOW CAN WATER BE FILTERED AND RECYCLED IN ORDER TO MEET THE DEMANDS OF THE CHANGING ENVIRONMENT AND A GROWING POPULATION ON EARTH?

According to the National Aeronautics and Space Administration (NASA), the average person on Earth uses up to 92 gallons (350 liters) of water a day. That's like drinking 1,400 glasses of water! But here's the problem: The world is facing a massive water shortage. Though 70 percent of the Earth's surface is covered with water, less than 2.5 percent of it can be used for drinking. Because of climate change and with the world's population exploding to more than 7.6 billion people, the competition for that water is fierce. Not everyone has equal access either.

There's another problem. The Earth's soil naturally filters water as it is absorbed into the ground as part of the water cycle. In many regions, due to pollution and harmful chemicals that have leeched into the soil, even drinkable groundwater has become too contaminated. For this reason, effective water-filtration devices are crucial to helping us conserve, clean, and recycle water so that everyone has enough to drink.

PROJECT
CREATE CLEAN WATER

Water-filtration devices come in all shapes and sizes. Use your imagination to plan, design, and construct one of your own. Then discuss ways in which your design could help solve a real-world problem.

- *Learn more about Earth's natural filtration system here: https://water.usgs.gov/edu/watercycleinfiltration.html. Then watch this video from NASA to gather more background information here: https://www.youtube.com/watch?v=BCjH3k5gODI.*
- *Begin your experiment by putting "dirty" water in a glass and mixing in dirt, glitter, or other similar materials.*

Have fun filling your glass with dirt and muck. For this experiment, the more contaminated the water is, the better.

- *Then design and create your own filtration system using household objects of your choosing. Some ideas include sand, coffee filters, rocks, rice, cotton balls, and a recyclable plastic bottle or glass funnel.*
- *Now test your filtration device by pouring the dirty water over it. Collect the "clean" water in a separate glass. If you have a drinking water test kit, use it to test the filtered sample alongside a glass of regular tap or bottled water.*
- *Analyze the data collected and use the information to refine and improve your design. Present the final design to the class.*
- *Brainstorm ideas for how your device can be used in day-to-day life. If it works, use it at home and report back!*

QUESTION: HOW HAVE INNOVATIVE THINKING AND NEW INVENTIONS IN ENGINEERING AND DESIGN ADVANCED SOCIETY AND BETTERED THE WORLD AT LARGE?

Innovators such as Margaret Knight, Steve Jobs, and Elon Musk have transformed the way humans view and interact with the environment. But adults aren't the only ones working on bettering the planet. In fact, thanks to programs like Discovery Education's Young Scientist Challenge, Google Science Fair, and Science Olympiad, kids and teens are designing breakthrough inventions of their own. Some are even winning cash.

On May 17, 2016, Jayden Madison and Ryan Mathews launched a pressurized water rocket during the tenth annual regional Elementary Science Olympiad at Chattanooga State Technical Community College.

The FIRST LEGO League Global Innovation Award is an engineering competition that invites students to design solutions for global challenges. In 2016, the top prize went to the Styro-Filter, a filtration device that takes Styrofoam and converts it into activated carbon that can be used to purify water. The patent-pending Styro-Filter, which was also a finalist for the 2016 Google Science Fair, could potentially reduce the nearly 2 billion pounds (907 million kilograms) of nonrecyclable Styrofoam that gets thrown away each year in the United States!

PROJECT
BECOME AN INVENTOR

The world is full of problems. Now's your time to lend a hand and fix one! Grab a partner and use your imaginations to channel your inner engineer and invent a unique product that could improve the world in some way.

- *Pick a famous engineer from history or today. Research some of his or her greatest inventions and read about how he or she got ideas off the ground. Some places to start include https://www.exploratorium.edu/explore and https://www.channelone.com/video-library.*
- *Think about your own life and the problems you see in the world. Choose one problem and interview people affected by it using audio or video recordings. Or read print or online news articles about the issue and keep detailed notes in your journal.*

- *With a partner, brainstorm possible solutions by designing and engineering your own invention. Factors to consider are materials, cost, time, and distribution requirements.*
- *If possible, build your invention and analyze your results. Then test, redesign, and rebuild it if necessary. Present your findings (and invention!) to the class. If the product can't be built, present your detailed design blueprint instead. Don't forget to explain why your invention will make the world a better place. If you're really inspired, enter a design competition like the FIRST LEGO League Global Innovation contest. You just might win!*

USEFUL TOOLS

The following is a list of some helpful project-based learning applications. All of them are free, offer free subscriptions, or have free trial versions:

- **Research:** Britannica School, Google Scholar, Todoist, EndNote, Digital Public Library of America, Citelighter, SweetSearch, Diigo
- **Science and Experiments:** NOVA, NASA Education, Smithsonian Science Education Center, CK-12, National Geographic Education, Curiosity Machine, Science Friday, HowStuffWorks, the Exploratorium, Science Toys, *Bill Nye the Science Guy*, Science News for Kids, BrainPOP, Project Noah
- **STEM Contests:** Intel Science Talent Search, Google Science Fair, ExploraVision, Science Olympiad, Young Scientist Challenge, Odyssey of the Mind, ProjectCSGirls Competition, Black Girls CODE Hackathon
- **Organization, Collaboration, and Communication:** Stormboard, Google Drive and Hangouts, Evernote, Pinterest, Livebinders, Slack, Asana
- **Mind and Concept Mapping:** Mindomo, Mindmeister, MindMup
- **Posters, Multimedia, and Publishing:** Glogster, Issuu, Scrivener
- **Digital Presentation/Project Portfolios:** Pathbrite, Google Slides, PowerPoint, PresentationTube, Prezi
- **Video:** YouTube, iMovie, LifeLogger, WeVideo, Magisto, TeleStory
- **Animation, Drawing, and Infographics:** Do Ink, Piktochat, Typrorama

GLOSSARY

acceleration The rate at which a moving object's speed increases.

biodiversity The existence of many different types of animals and plants in an environment.

dormant Not active but able to become active.

evolution The process by which changes in plants and animals happen over time.

exoplanet A planet that orbits a star that is outside our solar system.

extinct Wiped out; no longer existing.

hereditary Passed down from parent to offspring, or from generation to generation, as in genetic traits.

hypothesis A theory or educated guess about something, based on observation.

inertia Lack of movement.

inverse Opposite in position or direction; used to describe two things that are related in such a way that as one becomes larger the other becomes smaller.

manipulate To move or control something.

manometer A tool used to measure pressure.

mass The amount of matter in an object regardless of its volume or of any forces acting on it.

matter A substance made up of atoms and molecules that has mass and occupies physical space.

melanin A dark pigment in the hair, skin, and iris of the eye in people and animals.

meticulously Thoroughly; showing a lot of attention to detail.

oxidizes Combines with oxygen through a chemical process.

photodegradation The alteration of materials due to sunlight.

prediction A statement about what might happen in the future.

proportional Having parts that are the correct or fitting size in relation to each other.

radiation Energy given off by matter in the form of rays or high-speed particles.

relevant Closely connected to or having to do with an idea or something being considered.

tectonic plates The massive, slow-moving plates that make up Earth's surface.

thermohaline circulation Deep-ocean currents that are driven by differences in the water's density, which is controlled by temperature (thermo) and salinity (haline).

variable Something that changes or can be changed.

FOR MORE INFORMATION

Academy of Natural Sciences
1900 Benjamin Franklin Parkway
Philadelphia, PA 19103
(215) 299-1019
Website: https://www.ansp.org
Facebook: @AcademyofNaturalSciences
Instagram and Twitter: @AcadNatSci
Founded in 1812, the Academy of Natural Sciences at Drexel University is one of the oldest natural science research institutions and museums in the Americas. The museum is known for the massive *Tyrannosaurus rex* fossil that greets visitors at the entrance.

American Chemical Society
1155 Sixteenth Street NW
Washington, DC 20036
(800) 333-9511
Website: http://www.acs.org
Facebook: @AmericanChemicalSociety
Instagram and Twitter: @AmerChemSociety
Founded in 1876, this major scientific society provides tons of educational resources, including fun experiments to try and information about national chemistry week, the Chemistry Olympiad, and famous women scientists.

Canada Science and Technology Museum
2421 Lancaster Road
Ottawa, ON K1G 5A3
Canada
(613) 991-3044
Website: http://cstmuseum.techno-science.ca
Facebook, Instagram, and Twitter: @SciTechMuseum
Canada's largest museum dedicated to science and technology reopened in 2017 and features hands-on permanent, temporary, and traveling exhibits about life science, physical science, and more.

Engineering for Kids Foundation
1320 Central Park Boulevard,

Suite 201
Fredericksburg, VA 22401
(540) 940-2910
Website: http://engineeringforkids.com
Facebook: @EngineeringForKids
Twitter: @EFKCorp
Pintrest: @engineeringkids
With classes, camps, clubs, and other programs in the United States and more than twenty countries around the world, this organization brings middle school kids together to learn about a wide range of STEM (science, technology, engineering, and math) topics.

Exploratorium
Pier 15
(Embarcadero @ Green Street)
San Francisco, CA 94111
(415) 528-4444
Website: http://www.exploratorium.edu
Facebook and Twitter: @exploratorium
The Exploratorium packs more than six hundred interactive exhibits into six main galleries. The museum also hosts online exhibits featuring informative videos, apps, activities, and links to additional science-oriented websites.

Museum of Science & Industry
5700 S. Lake Shore Drive
Chicago, IL 60637
(773) 684-1414
Website: http://www.msichicago.org
Facebook, Instagram, and Twitter: @msichicago
Billing itself as the largest science museum in the Western Hemisphere with 400,000 square feet (37,000 square meters) of space, this museum in Chicago houses more than thirty-five thousand artifacts, an Omnimax theater, and science-related after-school learning programs.

National Aeronautics and Space Administration (NASA)

300 E Street SW, Suite 5R30
Washington, DC 20546
(202) 358-0001
Website: https://www.nasa.gov/audience/forstudents/index.html
Facebook and Instagram: @NASA
Twitter: @NASAedu
A US government agency responsible for studying the science and technology related to air and space. NASA features a dedicated website for students and educators and offers information about dozens of science- and space-related programs, projects, and volunteer opportunities throughout the year, as well as links to educational content.

Smithsonian National Air and Space Museum
Independence Avenue at Sixth Street SW
Washington, DC 20560
(202) 633-2214
Website: https://airandspace.si.edu
Facebook and Twitter: @airandspace
Instagram: @airandspacemuseum
This space museum is out of this world! It features twenty-two exhibition galleries covering the history of aviation, spaceflight, astronomy, and planetary science.

Youth Science Canada
1550 Kingston Road, Suite 213
Pickering, ON L1V 1C3
Canada
(416) 341-0040
Website: https://www.youthscience.ca
Facebook: @ysc.sjc
Instagram and Twitter: @ysc_sjc
This group is Canada's leading national organization dedicated to engaging youth in scientific inquiry and critical thinking.

FOR FURTHER READING

Ardley, Neil. *101 Great Science Experiments*. New York, NY: DK Publishing, 2014.

Birch, Hayley, Mun Keat Looi, and Colin Stuart. *Exploring the Mysteries of Science* (The STEM Guide to the Universe). New York, NY: Rosen Publishing, 2017.

Bortz, Fred. *Laws of Motion and Isaac Newton* (Revolutionary Discoveries of Scientific Pioneers). New York, NY: Rosen Publishing, 2014.

Brake, Mark. *The Big Earth Book.* Oakland, CA: Lonely Planet Kids, 2017.

Burling, Alexis. *Robert Boyle* (Leaders of the Scientific Revolution). New York, NY: Rosen Publishing, 2018.

Challoner, Jack. *Exploring the Mysteries of Genius and Invention* (The STEM Guide to the Universe). New York, NY: Rosen Publishing, 2017.

Challoner, Jack. *Smithsonian Maker Lab: 28 Super Cool Projects.* New York, NY: DK Publishing, 2016.

DK. *Smithsonian Science Year by Year: A Visual History, from Stone Tools to Space Travel.* New York, NY: DK Publishing, 2017.

Graves, Colleen, and Aaron Graves. *The Big Book of Makerspace Projects: Inspiring Makers to Experiment, Create, and Learn.* New York, NY: McGraw-Hill Education TAB, 2016.

Heinecke, Liz Lee. *STEAM Lab for Kids: 52 Creative Hands-On Projects Using Science, Technology, Engineering, Art, and Math*. Beverly, MA: Quarry Books, 2018.

Ignotofsky, Rachel. *Women in Science: 50 Fearless Pioneers Who Changed the World.* New York, NY: Ten Speed Press, 2016.

Kenney, Karen Latchana. *Energy Investigations* (Alternator Books: Key Questions in Physical Science). Minneapolis, MN: Lerner Publications, 2018.

Leidtke, Amy. *Leonardo's Art Workshop: Invent, Create, and Make STEAM Projects like a Genius*. Beverly, MA: Rockport Publishers, 2019.

Macaulay, David. *The Way Things Work Now.* Boston, MA: HMH Books for Young Readers, 2016.

Staley, Erin. *10 Great Makerspace Projects Using Science* (Using Makerspaces for School Projects). New York, NY: Rosen Publishing, 2018.

Trefil, James. *The Story of Innovation: How Yesterday's Discoveries Lead to Tomorrow's Breakthroughs*. Washington, DC: National Geographic, 2017.

Woodford, Chris. *Science: A Visual Encyclopedia.* New York, NY: DK Publishing, 2014.

Young, Karen Romano, and Matthew Rakola. *Try This! Extreme: 50 Fun & Safe Experiments for the Mad Scientist in You.* Washington, DC: National Geographic Children's Books, 2017.

BIBLIOGRAPHY

Chang, Kenneth. "A Nearby Earth-Size Planet May Have Conditions for Life." *New York Times*, November 15, 2017. https://www.nytimes.com/2017/11/15/science/planet-ross-128.html.

"Conditions That Support Life." University of Utah Genetic Science Learning Center. Retrieved February 26, 2018. http://learn.genetics.utah.edu/content/astrobiology/conditions.

Durani, Yamini. "Your Hair." KidsHealth.org, May 2015. http://kidshealth.org/en/kids/hair.html.

Fraser, Angela. "Describe Why Food Spoils." FoodSafetySite.com. Retrieved February 26, 2018. http://www.foodsafetysite.com/educators/competencies/general/spoilage/spg1.html.

Gaylord, Chris. "Marie Curie: How She Changed the World." *Christian Science Monitor*, November 7, 2011. https://www.csmonitor.com/Technology/Horizons/2011/1107/Marie-Curie-How-she-changed-the-world.

Gibbens, Sarah. "2017 Was the Hottest Year Yet in the World's Ocean." *National Geographic,* January 28, 2018. https://news.nationalgeographic.com/2018/01/hottest-year-record-global-warming-oceans-spd.

Kluger, Jeffrey. "Why Life on Mars May Be Impossible." *Time*, July 6, 2017. http://time.com/4845251/mars-life-toxins-microbes.

NASA. "The Thermohaline Circulation—the Great Ocean Conveyor Belt." Retrieved February 26, 2018. https://pmm.nasa.gov/education/videos/thermohaline-circulation-great-ocean-conveyor-belt.

National Geographic. "Freshwater Crisis." Retrieved February 26, 2018. https://www.nationalgeographic.com/environment/freshwater/freshwater-crisis.

NOAA National Centers for Environmental Information. "State of the Climate: Global Climate Report for Annual 2017." NOAA, January 2018. https://www.ncdc.noaa.gov/sotc/global/201713.

Peters, Adele. "In Puerto Rico, These Volunteers Are Dropping Supplies by Parachute." *Fast Company*, October 13, 2017. https://www.fastcompany.com/40478304/in-puerto-rico-these-volunteers-are-dropping-supplies-by-parachute.

Peters, Adele. "10 Clever Student Inventions That Could Reduce Our Waste." *Fast Company*, June 9, 2016. https://www.fastcompany.com/3060571/10-clever-student-inventions-that-could-reduce-our-waste.

Rasmussen, Carol. "Our Living Planet Shapes the Search for Life Beyond Earth." NASA, November 15, 2017. https://www.nasa.gov/feature/jpl/our-living-planet-shapes-the-search-for-life-beyond-earth.

Time staff. "The 25 Best Inventions of 2017." *Time*, December 1, 2017. http://time.com/5023212/best-inventions-of-2017.

USGS Water Science School. "Infiltration—the Water Cycle." USGS, December 15, 2016. https://water.usgs.gov/edu/watercycleinfiltration.html.

U.S.NRC. "Uses of Radiation." October 2, 2017. https://www.nrc.gov/about-nrc/radiation/around-us/uses-radiation.html.

Wild, Flint, ed. "What Is Earth?" NASA, October 4, 2017. https://www.nasa.gov/audience/forstudents/5-8/features/nasa-knows/what-is-earth-58.html.

INDEX

ABOUT THE AUTHOR

Alexis Burling has published numerous books and articles for kids and teens on a variety of topics ranging from current events and career advice to biographies of famous people. She also loves doing science experiments. In fact, when she was in seventh grade, she and her science partner won the egg-drop contest by designing an unbreakable enclosure with top secret cushioning. The egg inside survived after it was dropped from the roof of her school! Of course, Burling remembered to take copious notes in her journal. She lives with her husband in Portland, Oregon.

PHOTO CREDITS

Cover, p. 1 Hill Street Studios/Blend Images/Getty Images; p. 3 Ollyy /Shutterstock.com; p. 4 Pressmaster/Shutterstock.com; p. 5 Pictorial Press Ltd/Alamy Stock Photo; p. 6 Wavebreakmedia/Shutterstock .com; p. 9 De Agostini Picture Library/Getty Images; pp. 12, 47 Africa Studio/Shutterstock.com; p. 14 Denis Val/Shutterstock.com; p. 15 Claudia Paulussen/Shutterstock.com; p. 18 Gertan/Shutterstock.com; p. 20 Monkey Business Images/Shutterstock.com; p. 22 Sirtravelalot /Shutterstock.com; pp. 24, 35 Bettmann/Getty Images; p. 26 CGN089 /Shutterstock.com; p. 28 Basnik/iStock/Thinkstock; p. 32 Photobank Gallery/Shutterstock.com; p. 33 Andrew Fox/Corbis Documentary /Getty Images; p. 39 Fuse/Corbis/Getty Images; p. 42 Riopatuca /Shutterstock.com; p. 45 Boris Yaro/Los Angeles Times/Getty Images; p. 49 © AP Images.

Design: Nelson Sá; Layout: Ellina Litmanovich; Editor: Amelie von Zumbusch; Photo Researcher: Sherri Jackson